Grandma and Grandpa Need Help with the Puppies

Reneé Tamburello

Our family favorite cookie recipe enclosed on page 25

Copyright © 2023 Reneé Tamburello
All rights reserved
First Edition

PAGE PUBLISHING
Conneaut Lake, PA

First originally published by Page Publishing 2023

ISBN 979-8-88654-954-6 (hc)
ISBN 979-8-88654-951-5 (digital)

Printed in the United States of America

This book was written for all dog lovers
but most of all my six grandchildren:
Riley Tamburello
Dylan Tamburello
Josephine Tamburello
Anthony Tamburello V
Tommy Tamburello
and
Maverick Tamburello

I feel blessed to have a beautiful, wonderful family. I would like to thank my two sons, Anthony IV and Steven Tamburello, for giving me such a happy life.

Grandma and Grandpa have two small pocket poodles. Tina is silver and only three pounds. She is going to have puppies soon. Sonny is a black pocket poodle. He is only five pounds. He is the puppies' father.

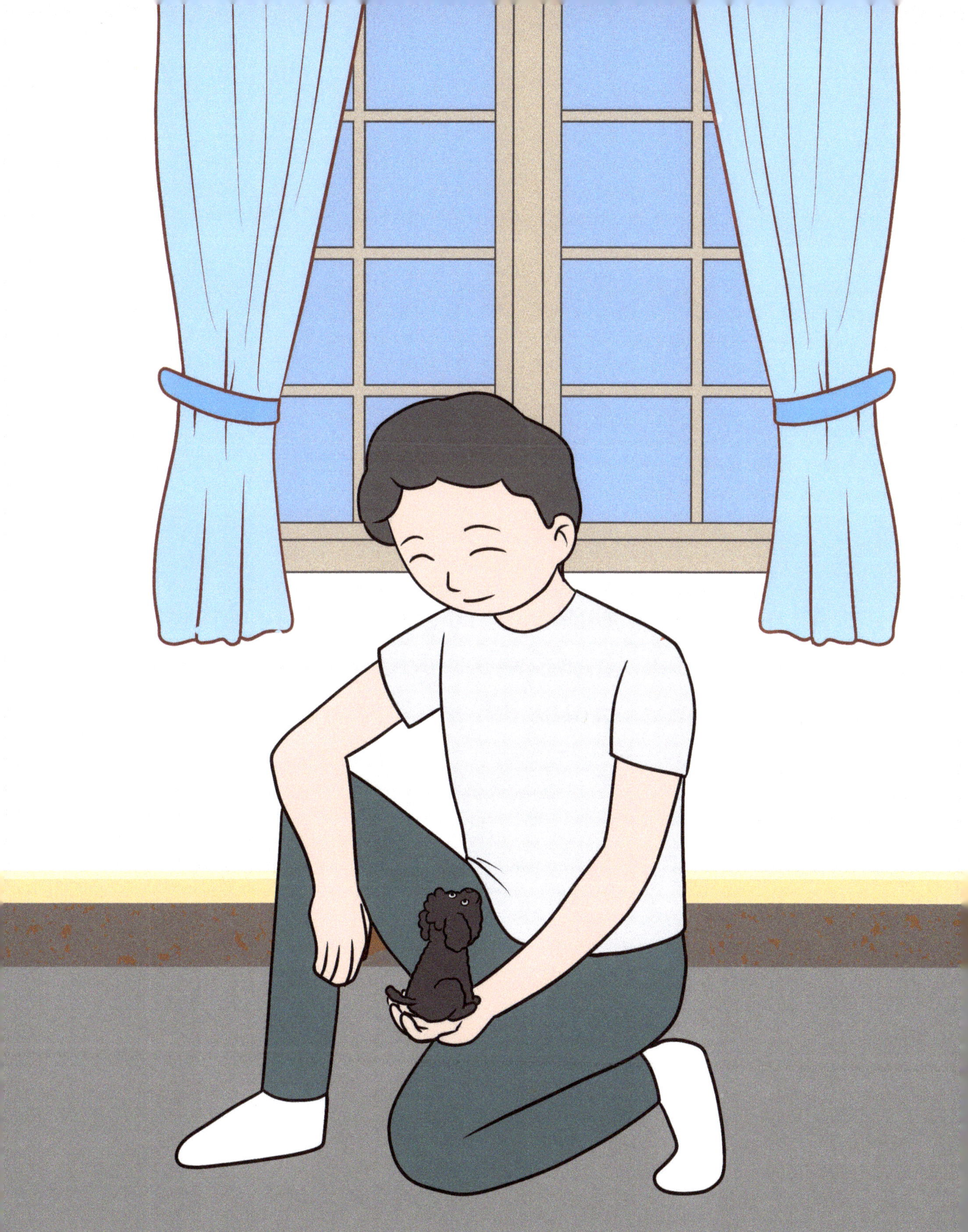

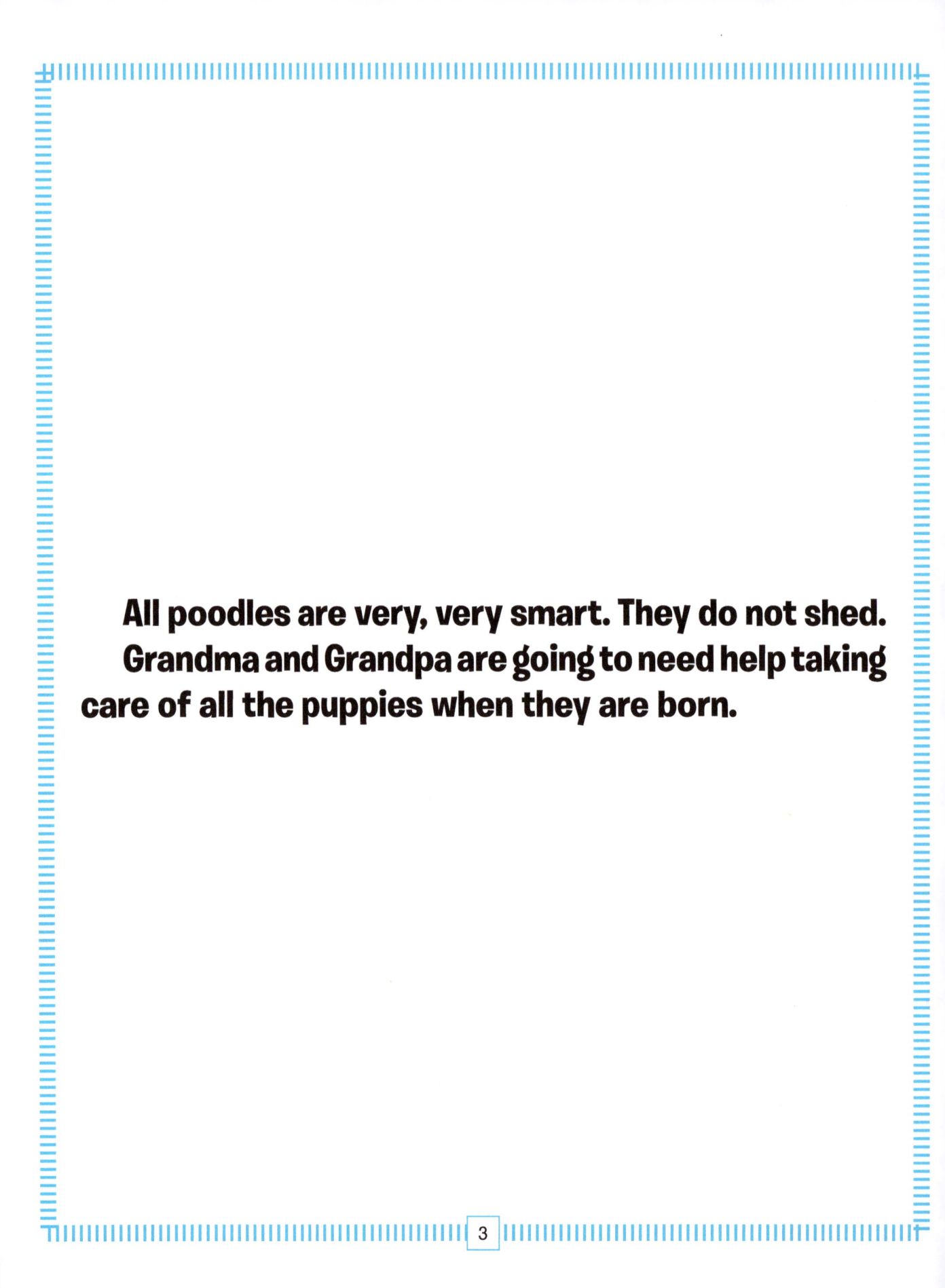

All poodles are very, very smart. They do not shed. Grandma and Grandpa are going to need help taking care of all the puppies when they are born.

4

Finally, the puppies are here! We have to count all the puppies as they are born. There are many. "I counted eight puppies," said Grandma. Four girls and four boys.

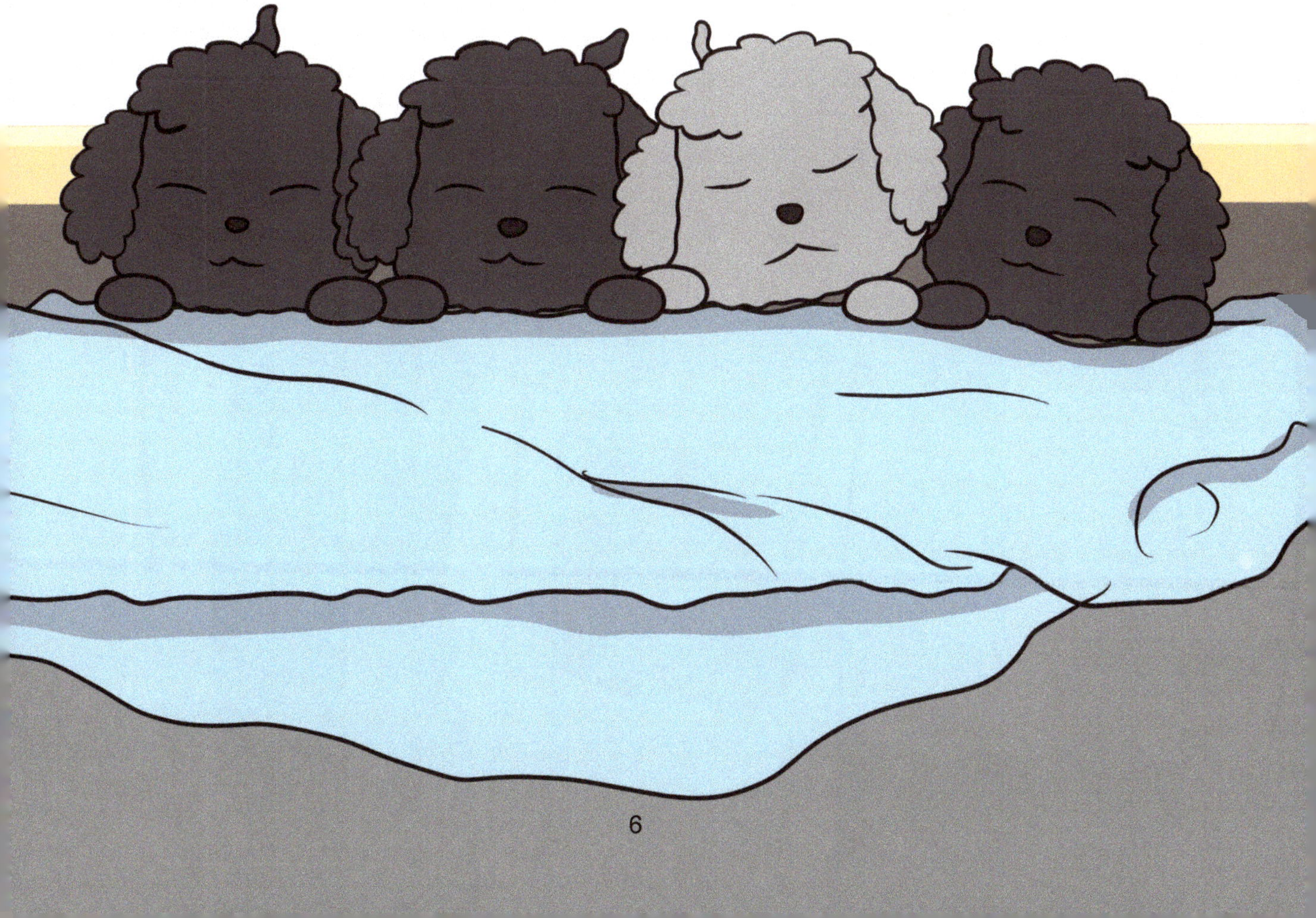

Grandma goes to get her phone. She needs to call up both her sons, Anthony and Steven. She needs them to bring over all six of her grandchildren–Riley, Dylan, Josephine, Anthony, Tommy, and Maverick. They can help with the puppies.

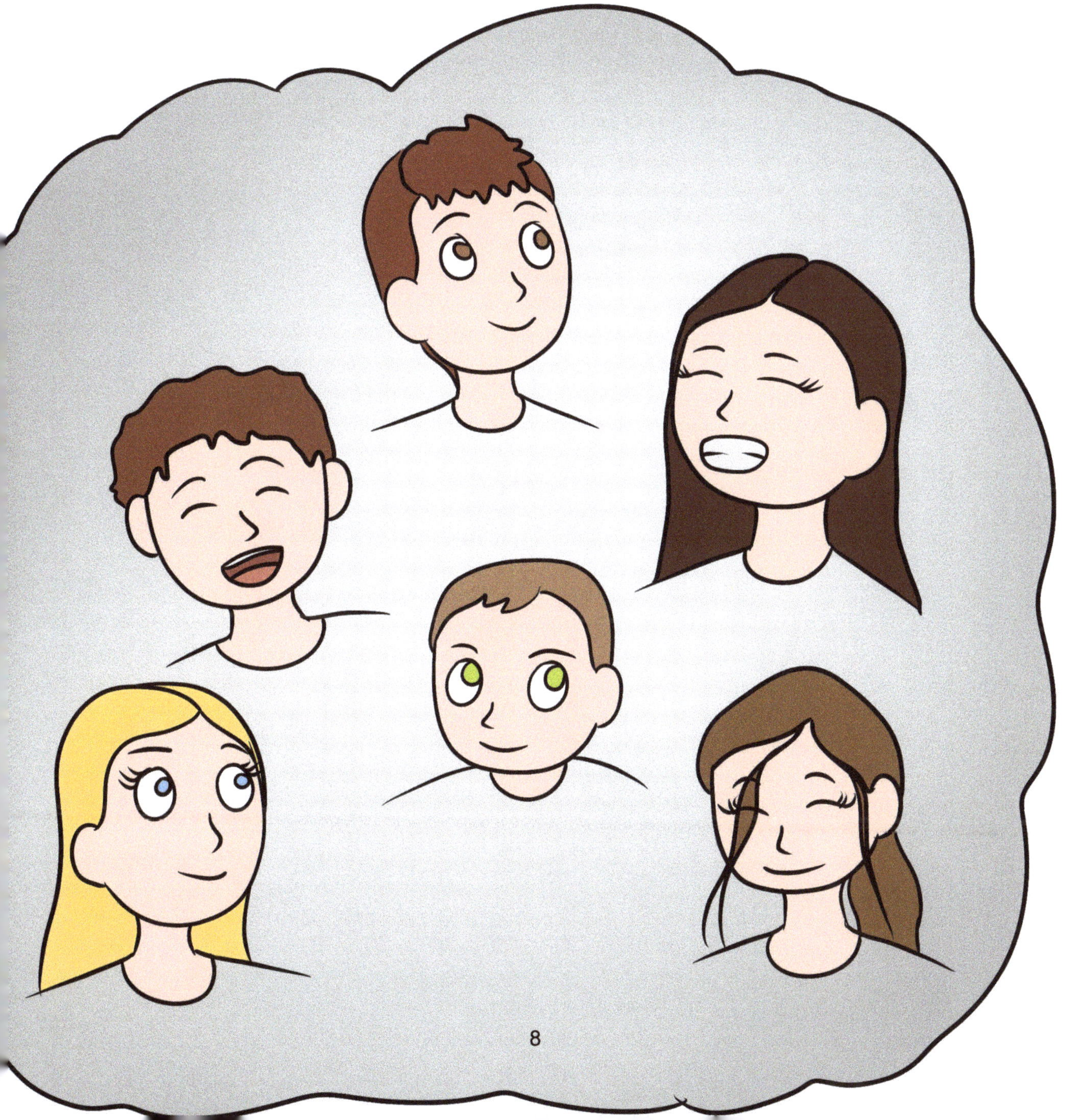

All six grandchildren come over to help give the puppies a bath. Riley, Dylan, Josephine, Anthony, Tommy, and Maverick line up, holding one puppy each.

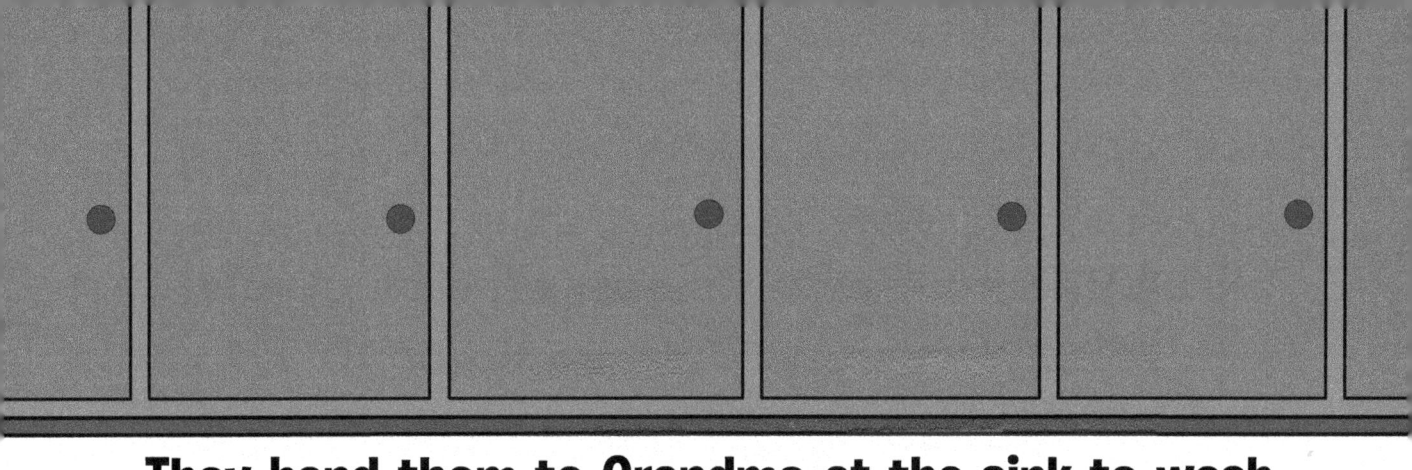

They hand them to Grandma at the sink to wash them. Grandma also washes Sonny and Tina, the puppies' mom and dad.

Riley, Dylan, and Josephine dry off their puppies first. Then Anthony, Tommy, and Maverick dry off the rest of the puppies. They put the puppies down for a nap.

While the puppies are sleeping, all the grandchildren help Grandma and Grandpa put up the Christmas tree. Grandma bakes cookies for everyone. Peanut butter cookies are their favorite.

Pocket poodles are very small. So small they can fit in your pocket. They stay small their entire lives. They don't eat much and are easy to care for.

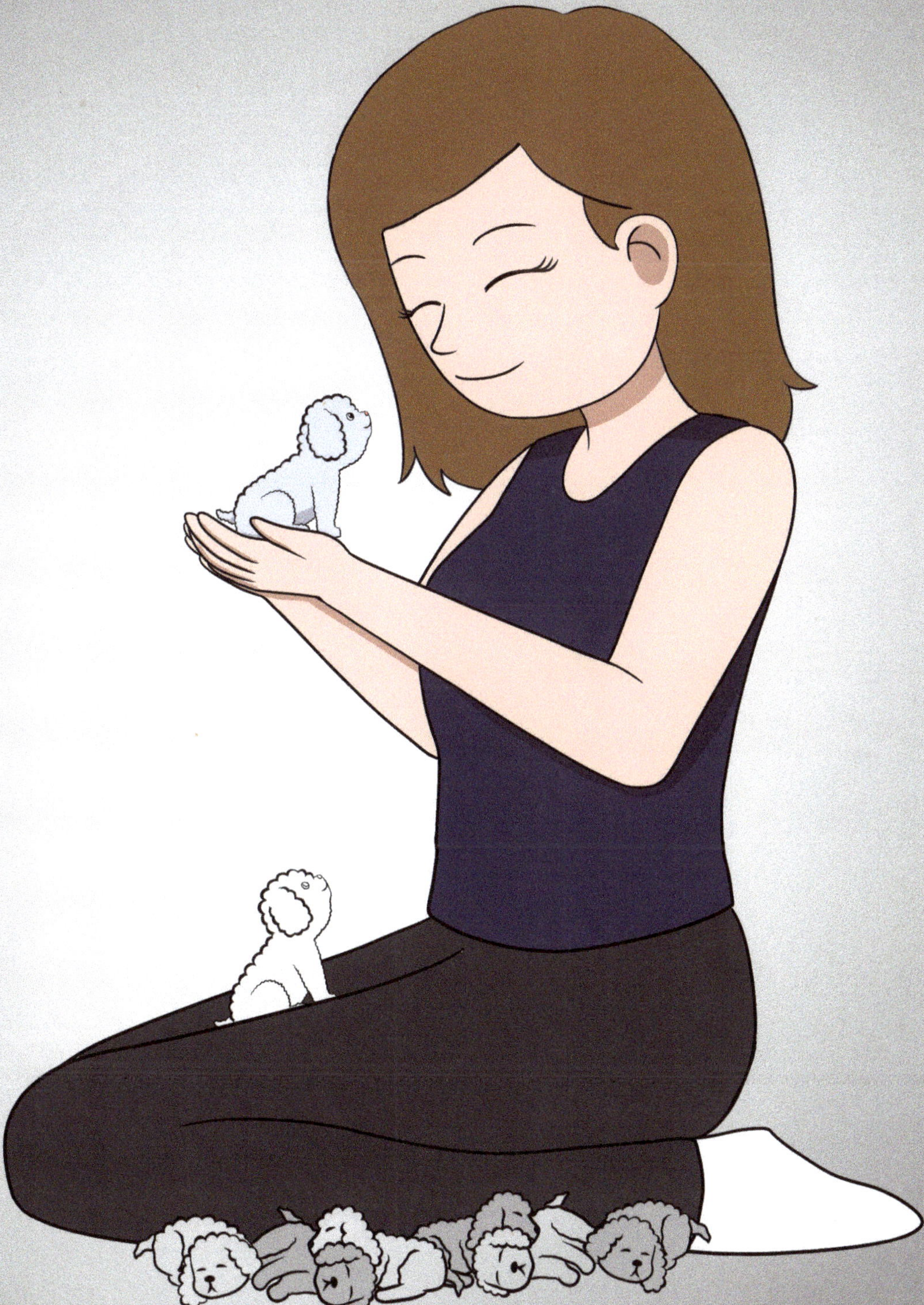

15

Spring comes and it is Easter. All of Grandma and Grandpa's grandchildren come over and take the puppies outside to play on the grass. Riley, Dylan, Josephine, Anthony, Tommy, and Maverick have an Easter egg hunt.

Poodles are water dogs. When summer comes, all the poodles have fun in the pool with all six grandchildren, Grandma, Grandpa, and Anthony and Steven, their sons.

18

It is fall, and Halloween has come before we know it. All the grandchildren come over to dress up the puppies in costume and bring them to trick or treat with them. It is fun.

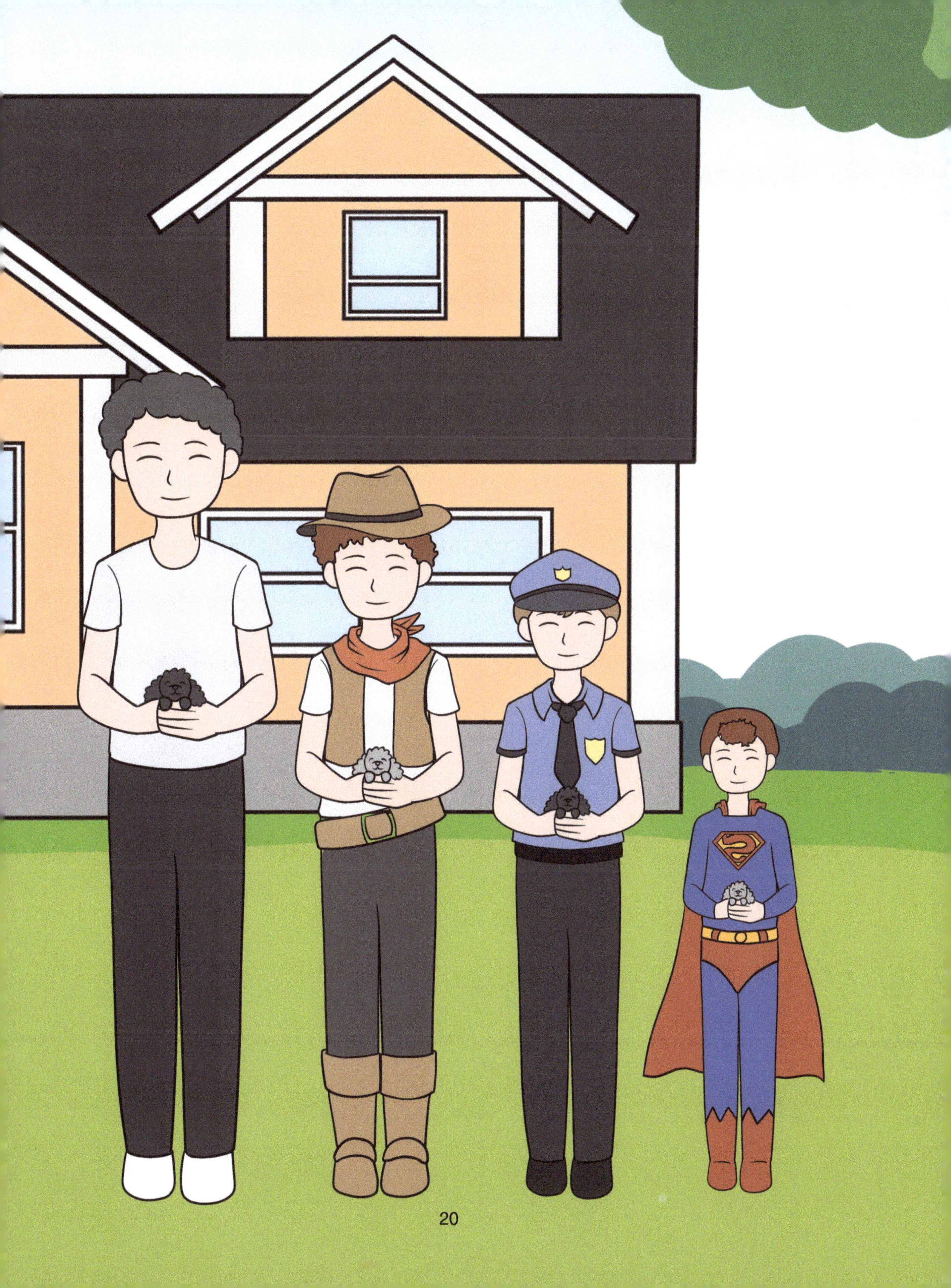

Thanksgiving is here, and our family has a lot to be thankful for. Grandma and Grandpa are happy they are blessed with two wonderful sons, six beautiful grandchildren, and all of their puppies to love.

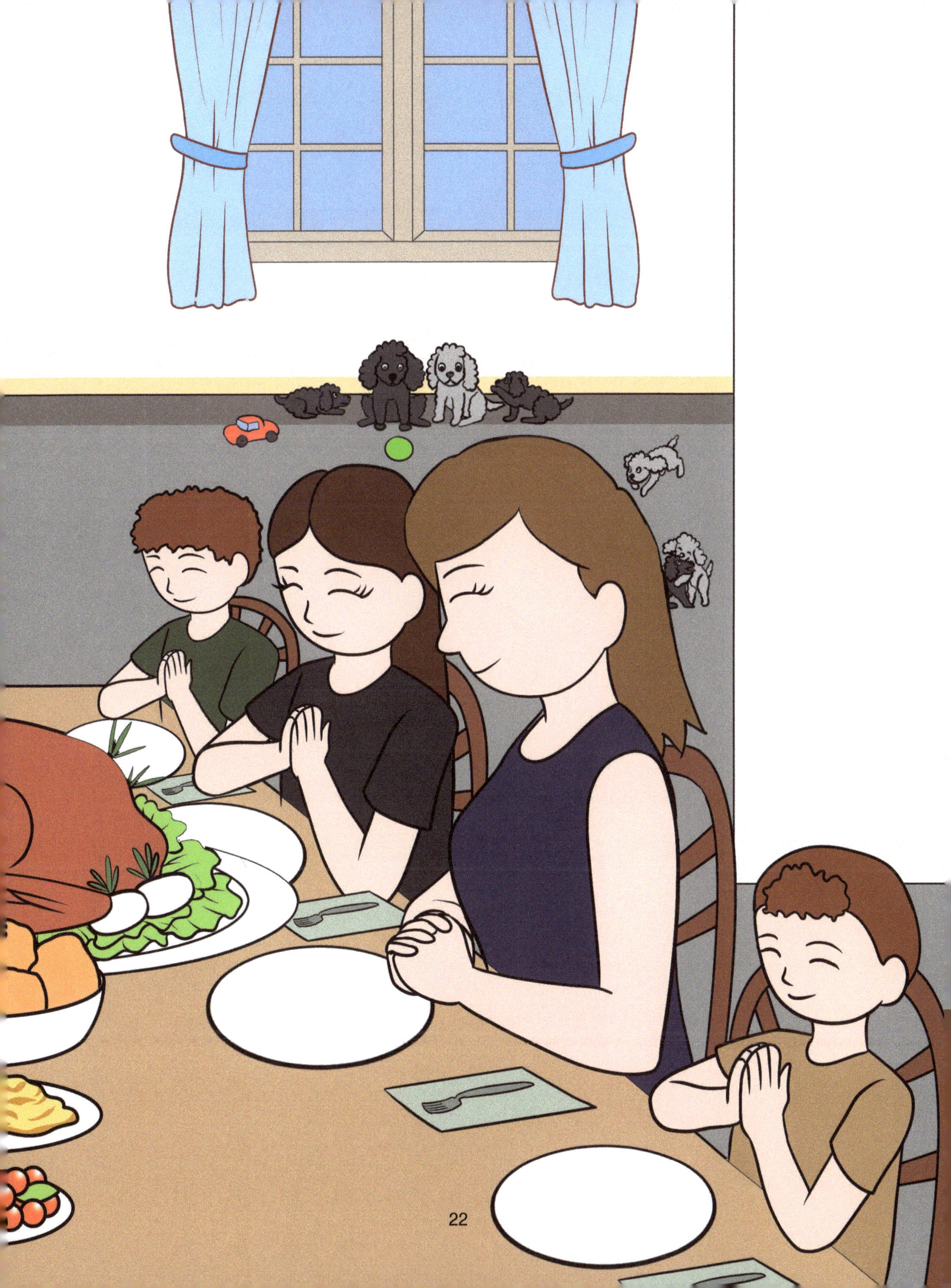

23

December is here and it is almost Christmas. The puppies are one year old. Grandma is making special cupcakes for the puppies and all her grandchildren.

Recipe: Grandma's Peanut Butter Cookies

1/2 cup of butter (one stick)
1/2 cup smooth peanut butter
1/3 cup white sugar
1/3 cup brown sugar
1 egg
1/2 teaspoon vanilla
1/2 teaspoon baking soda
1 1/4 cup unbleached white flour

Pre-heat oven at 350 degrees.
Mix all ingredients. Spoon onto pan.
Bake for 10 to 12 minutes.

From:

Serves:

©ME•E•Inc. CURRENT USA, Inc.

Grandma and Grandpa can't wait to go on vacation with their children, grandchildren, dogs, and puppies to some place with a large park.

The end.

About the Author

Reneé Christine Tamburello was born Reneé Christine Costabile in Brooklyn, New York. She moved to Lindenhurst, New York, with her family when she was ten years old. She attended Our Lady of Perpetual Help School. After she graduated high school, she went to beauty school and became a cosmetologist. She and her husband married on May 1, 1982, at OLPH Church. The couple shares two sons: Anthony and Steven. She and her husband also have six wonderful grandchildren–Riley, Dylan, Josephine, Anthony, Tommy, and Maverick. Reneé feels blessed to have a wonderful family.